# more
# TAKE 5 QUILTS

# more TAKE 5 QUILTS

## 16 new quick and easy projects

Kathy Brown

Martingale®
Create with Confidence

## Mission Statement
Dedicated to providing quality products and service to inspire creativity.

## Credits
President & CEO: Tom Wierzbicki

Editor in Chief: Mary V. Green

Design Director: Paula Schlosser

Managing Editor: Karen Costello Soltys

Technical Editor: Ellen Pahl

Copy Editor: Marcy Heffernan

Production Manager: Regina Girard

Cover & Text Designer: Shelly Garrison

Illustrator: Robin Strobel

Photographer: Brent Kane

More Take 5 Quilts: 16 New Quick and Easy Projects
© 2012 by Kathy Brown

Martingale®
19021 120th Ave. NE, Suite 102
Bothell, WA 98011 USA
ShopMartingale.com

Printed in China
17 16 15 14 13 12      8 7 6 5 4 3 2

**Library of Congress Cataloging-in-Publication Data is available upon request.**

ISBN: 978-1-60468-137-6

# CONTENTS

I've always been a believer in making memories as you journey through life. As I've grown older, I realize more and more just how special these memories are. Whether precious childhood events, treasured family moments, or special times with friends, the memories you gather along the way are what comfort you, bring you guidance, and see you through good times and bad. You grow with your memories, reflect, and continue to make more.

As I began working on this book, I reflected on my journey with the "Take 5" concept and the memories I've made along the way. What started out as a simple premise—take five minutes, choose five fabrics, and in five hours you can make a quilt top—has basically remained the same. Over time, I've stretched the time clock a bit when choosing those fabrics—but not by much! And, yes, I've added a neutral fabric or two in the mix so that the five fabrics are showcased against a background. Yes, I've stretched the time it takes to make a Take 5 quilt in some instances so that we could make a larger quilt or incorporate more intricate designs. Yes, I've added just a touch of appliqué to the quilts, as in "Take 5 . . . Connects the Dots" (page 22). What's a quilting life without a little appliqué in it? And, yes, I've even created a Take 5 quilt that requires you to cut out all of the fabrics individually, rather than in a stack, as in "Take 5 . . . Picks a Basket of Blooms" (page 70). It still has five fabrics, doesn't it?

What started out as a single pattern, however, has not remained so. The original Take 5 pattern took flight and began a journey that I never dreamed would happen. One individual pattern turned into 12, and then blossomed into two books with 31 additional quilts. Along the way, many memories have been forged. I remember the first quilt I ever made, and how scared I was to be cutting into those beautiful fabrics and doing this all on my own—it was the original

Take 5. I remember the first quilt class I ever taught, and how nervous I was to be teaching a class of women how to make a quilt—it was the Take 5 pattern. I remember the first quilt I quilted on a long-arm machine, and how I didn't want to screw it up—it was a Take 5. I remember the first quilt I ever gave away as a gift (to my dad)—it was a Take 5. I remember the youngest student I ever taught—she was eight years old, cute as a bug, and she made a quilt in just a little over five hours—it was a Take 5. I remember the oldest student I ever taught—she was 94 and cute as a bug too—and she made a quilt in just *under* five hours! It was a Take 5! I remember walking into a quilt shop and seeing one of my quilts on display for the first time, and it was a Take 5. I remember the times, the dates, the places, the sights, the sounds, the smells, the feelings of pride, of accomplishment, of joy, the dismay when things didn't go just right, and the delight when they did—and they were all Take 5 quilts! I remember all these things and many, many more from this Take 5 journey.

But those are my memories through this journey with the Take 5 quilts. It's time for you to create some memories of your own, right here and now. Which Take 5 quilt will you choose to make? Will it be a fun-loving, modern dot-to-dot quilt that you give to a very special child, crafting memories for them that will last a lifetime? Or will you choose a time-honored traditional Spool block or Tumbler block to create lasting memories? And what about the fabrics? Will you choose modern, retro, reproduction, classic, novelty, juvenile, or romantic prints? In the end, whatever quilt you choose, whatever fabrics you choose, and for whatever reason you make those choices, your journey has begun. So let that journey be a good one, and enjoy it in good health with a warm heart!

— Kathy

Designed by Kathy Brown; pieced by Linda Reed; quilted by Carol Hilton

# Backyard barbecues

with family and friends were a summertime staple when I was growing up. The entire day was spent cleaning house, mowing the yard, and preparing mouthwatering dishes in anticipation of everyone's arrival in the late afternoon. The barbecue was cleaned and brought out to its place of honor while brightly colored strings of Chinese lanterns were strung from tree to tree as final preparations were made. In those moments, the sights, the sounds, and the smells all mingled with the warmth and comfort of treasured friends gathered together.

As I assembled the fabrics for this quilt, the memories of those special summer days came rushing back to wrap me in their warmth. I hope this quilt will spark a remembrance of special occasions with family and friends for you as well.

## MATERIALS

*Yardage is based on 42"-wide fabric.*

¾ yard of blue print for blocks

¾ yard of green print for blocks

¾ yard of red print for blocks

1 yard of black print for blocks

1⅓ yards of cream print for block backgrounds

3⅜ yards of black print for sashing, inner border, outer border, and binding

½ yard of red print for middle border

4⅞ yards of fabric for backing

79" x 88" piece of batting

## CUTTING THE LAYERED PIECES

Refer to "Rotary Cutting" on page 75 to stack the fabrics and straighten the edges. Refer to the cutting diagram below to cut the layered fabrics as indicated, cutting in order from left to right.

**From *each* of the ¾-yard pieces, cut:**
21 rectangles, 3½" x 12½"

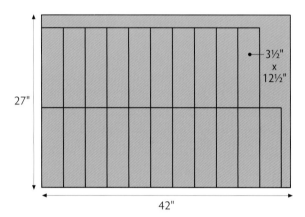

## CUTTING THE REMAINING PIECES

**From the black print for blocks, cut:**
14 strips, 1" x 42"; crosscut into 40 rectangles, 1" x 12½"

12 strips, 1½" x 42"; crosscut into 40 rectangles, 1½" x 6½"

**From the black print for sashing, borders, and binding, cut:**
5 strips, 1½" x 4"; crosscut into 15 rectangles, 1½" x 12½"

8 strips, 1½" x 42"

8 strips, 8½" x 42"

8 strips, 2½" x 42"

**From the cream print, cut:**
8 strips, 1½" x 42"; crosscut into 80 rectangles, 1½" x 3½"

8 strips, 3½" x 42"; crosscut into 80 squares, 3½" x 3½"

**From the red print for middle border, cut:**
8 strips, 1½" x 42"

## CONSTRUCTING THE LANTERN BLOCKS

1. Separate the 3½" x 12½" rectangles and stack them in groups so that you have three different groupings: green, blue, and red prints.

2. Mark a diagonal line from corner to corner on the wrong side of all of the cream 3½" squares.

3. Next to each of the green and blue stacks, place 14 each of the black 1" x 12½" and 1½" x 6½" rectangles. Add 28 each of the cream 1½" x 3½" rectangles and 3½" squares to these stacks.

4. Next to the red fabric stack, place 12 each of the black 1" x 12½" and 1½" x 6½" rectangles. Add 24 each of the cream 1½" x 3½" strips and 3½" squares to the red stack. You'll have three red strips left over. Put these in your fabric stash for future use.

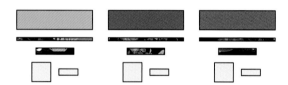

5. Sew three green 3½" x 12½" strips together with two black 1" x 12½" strips as shown. Press.

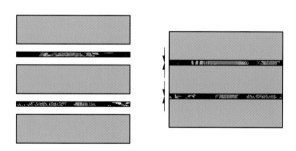

6. Sew a marked cream 3½" square diagonally on each of the four corners of the green unit as shown. Trim the excess fabric ¼" from the sewn line. Press the seam allowances toward the corners.

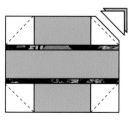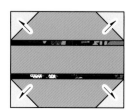

**7** Sew a cream 1½" x 3½" strip to each end of a black 1½" x 6½" strip as shown. Make two of these units.

Make 2.

**8** Sew units from step 7 to the top and bottom of the unit from step 6. Make seven green blocks.

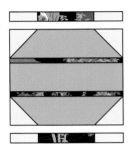 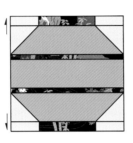

**9** Repeat steps 5–8 with the remaining stacks to make a total of seven blue blocks and six red blocks.

## ASSEMBLING THE QUILT TOP

**1** Working on a design wall or other flat surface, arrange the completed blocks and black-print sashing strips in five rows of four blocks each as shown in the assembly diagram. Sew the blocks and sashing strips into rows. Press the seam allowances toward the sashing in every other row and toward the blocks in alternate rows.

**2** Sew the rows together to form the quilt top. Press the seam allowances in one direction.

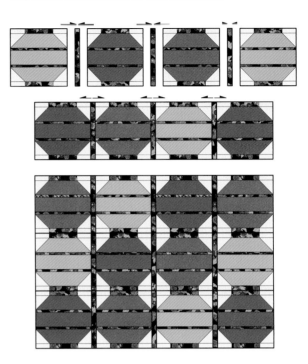

**3** Referring to "Adding Borders" on page 76, sew two black 1½"-wide inner-border strips together to make one long strip. Repeat to make four long strips.

**4** Sew the inner borders to the quilt top. Press.

**5** Repeat steps 3 and 4 to add the red middle borders and the black 8½"-wide outer borders.

## FINISHING

**1** Refer to "Completing the Quilt" on page 76 to layer the quilt top, batting, and backing. Quilt as desired.

**2** Sew the black 2½"-wide binding strips together to form one continuous strip and bind the quilt.

Designed by Kathy Brown; pieced by Linda Reed; quilted by Carol Hilton

**Finished Quilt:** 67½" x 82½" — **Finished Block:** 7½" x 7½"

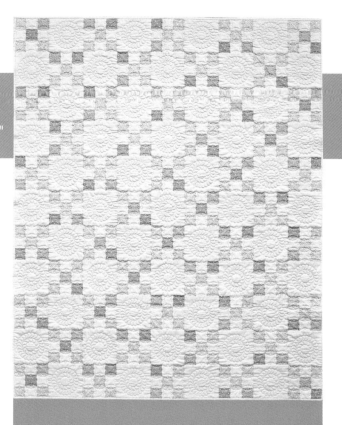

# Going to stay with

my great-aunt and great-uncle during the summer was always a great treat for my brothers and me. While we lived in a large subdivision in the suburbs, they lived on a working cattle farm! A sprawling farmhouse, cattle pastures as far as the eye could see, a stable with horses just waiting for us to ride them, and a barn complete with milk cows and chickens were a delight for our senses. On Saturdays, my great-aunt would take us to the general store where she would buy supplies—usually flour, sugar, and grains bought in bulk. On some of these occasions, she was lucky enough to purchase these bulk items in feedsacks, which by the early 1960s were becoming less and less plentiful. Eventually, the feedsacks were cut into squares and remade into beautiful quilts hand stitched by my aunt.

The reproduction fabrics in this quilt reminded me of those treasured trips to the general store with my great-aunt, and of all the beautiful quilts we would snuggle under each night. May this quilt bring back treasured memories of days gone by for you too.

## MATERIALS

*Yardage is based on 42"-wide fabric.*

½ yard of pink print for blocks

½ yard of blue print for blocks

½ yard of green print for blocks

½ yard of purple print for blocks

½ yard of yellow print for blocks

4⅓ yards of muslin for blocks

¾ yard of muslin for binding

5⅛ yards of fabric for backing

76" x 91" piece of batting

## CUTTING THE LAYERED PIECES

Refer to "Rotary Cutting" on page 75 to stack the fabrics and straighten the edges. Refer to the cutting diagram below to cut the layered fabrics as indicated.

From *each of the* ½-yard pieces, cut:

5 strips, 3" x 42"

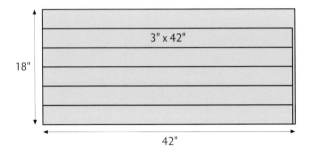

## CUTTING THE REMAINING PIECES

From the muslin for blocks, cut:

20 strips, 3" x 42"

49 squares, 8" x 8"

From the muslin for binding, cut:

9 strips, 2½" x 42"

## CONSTRUCTING THE BLOCKS

1. Separate the 3" x 42" strips and stack them in groups so that you have five different groupings: pink, blue, green, purple, and yellow prints. Place all of the muslin 3" x 42" strips in a stack and the muslin 8" x 8" squares in another stack next to the colored strips.

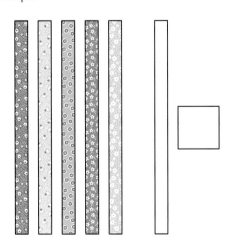

2. Sew a muslin 3" x 42" strip and two colored 3" x 42" strips together as shown to make a strip set. Make two strip sets in each of the following combinations: pink, muslin, purple; green, muslin, pink; purple, muslin, yellow; green, muslin, blue; blue, muslin, yellow. Press all the seam allowances toward the colored strips

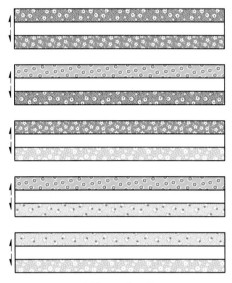

Make 2 of each.

3. Make one strip set in each of the following combinations: muslin, pink, muslin; muslin, green, muslin; muslin, purple, muslin; muslin, blue, muslin; muslin, yellow, muslin. Press the seam allowances toward the colored strips.

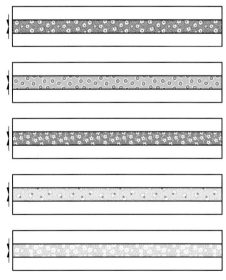

Make 1 of each.

④ From each strip set, cut 10 segments, 3" wide.

⑤ Stack all of the matching segments together into piles. Divide the stacks of segments that are color-muslin-color into two stacks, one arranged as shown, and one turned 180° so that the matching colors are on opposite ends.

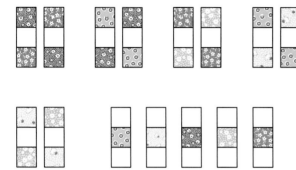

⑥ Sew a muslin-color-muslin segment between two color-muslin-color segments to make a Nine Patch block. Make 10 blocks each of the five color combinations shown.

Make 10 of each.

## ASSEMBLING THE QUILT TOP

① Using a design wall or other flat surface, arrange the completed Nine Patch blocks and muslin squares in 11 rows of nine blocks each, alternating the blocks as shown in the quilt diagram.

② Sew the blocks into rows. Press the seam allowances toward the muslin squares. Sew the blocks together. Press.

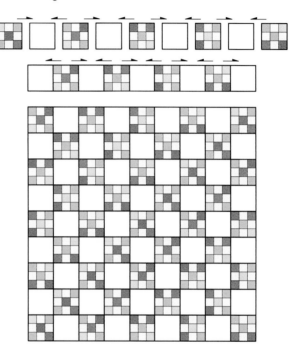

## FINISHING

① Refer to "Completing the Quilt" on page 76 to layer the quilt top, batting, and backing. Quilt as desired.

② Sew the binding strips together to form one continuous strip and bind the quilt.

Designed by Kathy Brown; pieced by Linda Reed; quilted by Carol Hilton

**Finished Quilt:** 74" x 88" — **Finished Block:** 14" x 14"

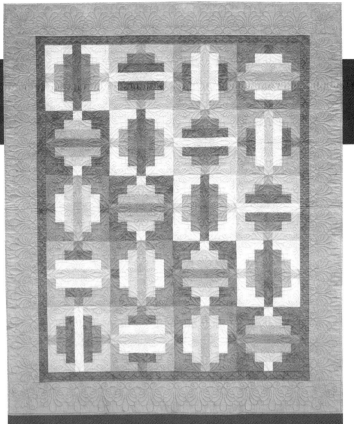

As anyone who has ever traveled through southern Louisiana knows, we here in bayou country love our coffee, and we love it strong. Many a friendship has been forged over a cup of French drip; a relationship mended over cups of steaming café-au-lait; or days passed in harmony while sipping an afternoon mug of coffee and chicory. Having been born in the mid-1950s, I was the product of grandparents and parents who drank coffee all day long, every day. It was the custom at that time to fill a baby bottle or sippy cup halfway with milk, top it off with cool coffee, lace it liberally with sugar, and give it to the bébés to drink. And drink coffee milk we did! It's no wonder that I grew up loving the taste of coffee, and I can drink it from morning till night and back again!

The color range of the hand-dyed muslin fabrics used in this quilt remind me of the coffees in my home state, from the dark, rich, bold hues to the creamy, sugary coffee-milk tones. Cup of coffee, anyone?

## MATERIALS

*Yardage is based on 42"-wide fabric.*

1 yard of off-white solid for blocks

1 yard of cream solid for blocks

1 yard of beige solid for blocks

1 yard of tan solid for blocks

1 yard of brown solid for blocks

⅔ yard of brown solid for inner border

2⅝ yards of beige solid for outer border and binding

5½ yards of fabric for backing

82" x 96" piece of batting

## CUTTING THE LAYERED PIECES

Refer to "Rotary Cutting" on page 75 to stack the fabrics and straighten the edges. Refer to the cutting diagram below to cut the layered fabrics as indicated, cutting in order from left to right.

**From *each* of the 1-yard pieces, cut:**

24 squares, 2½" x 2½"

16 rectangles, 2½" x 4½"

24 rectangles, 2½" x 6½"

8 rectangles, 2½" x 10½"

4 rectangles, 2½" x 14½"

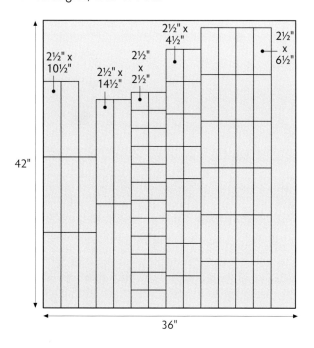

## CUTTING THE REMAINING PIECES

**From the brown solid for inner border, cut:**
8 strips, 2½" x 42"

**From the beige solid for outer border and binding, cut:**
8 strips, 7½" x 42"

9 strips, 2½" x 42"

## CONSTRUCTING THE BLOCKS

1. Separate the fabrics, stacking all of the same-fabric rectangles and squares into piles so that you'll have five different groupings: off-white, cream, beige, tan, and brown solids.

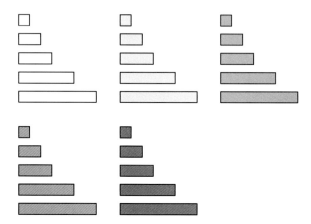

2. Sew off-white 2½" x 6½" rectangles to opposite sides of a cream 2½" square. Make two and set aside.

Make 2.

3. Sew off-white 2½" x 4½" rectangles to opposite ends of a beige 2½" x 6½" rectangle as shown. Make two and set aside.

Make 2.

4. Sew off-white 2½" squares to opposite ends of a tan 2½" x 10½" rectangle as shown. Make two and set aside.

Make 2.

5. Sew a unit each from steps 2, 3, and 4 together as shown. Make two of these block sections.

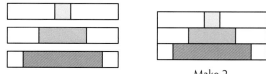

Make 2.

**6** Sew a section from step 5 to each side of a brown 2½" x 14½" rectangle as shown to complete the block.

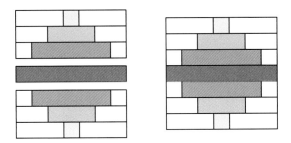

**7** Repeat steps 2–6 to make four blocks using off-white pieces. Then repeat the steps using the cream, beige, tan, and then brown pieces in place of the off-white. The fabric positions will shift with each variation of the first block. Make four blocks each of the five color combinations as shown.

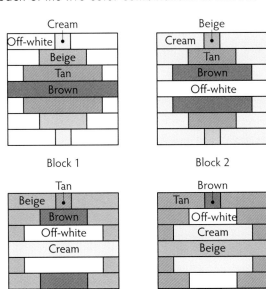

Cream

| Off-white | • |
|---|---|
| Beige | |
| Tan | |
| Brown | |

Block 1

Beige

| Cream | • |
|---|---|
| Tan | |
| Brown | |
| Off-white | |

Block 2

Tan

| Beige | • |
|---|---|
| Brown | |
| Off-white | |
| Cream | |

Block 3

Brown

| Tan | • |
|---|---|
| Off-white | |
| Cream | |
| Beige | |

Block 4

Off-white

| Brown | • |
|---|---|
| Cream | |
| Beige | |
| Tan | |

Block 5

## ASSEMBLING THE QUILT TOP

**1** Using a design wall or other flat surface, arrange the completed blocks as shown in the assembly diagram. Sew the blocks together into rows, pressing the seam allowances in opposite directions from row to row. Sew the rows together.

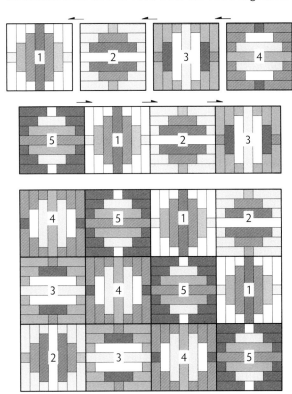

**2** Referring to "Adding Borders" on page 76, sew two brown inner-border strips together to make one long strip. Repeat to make four long strips.

**3** Sew the inner borders to the quilt top. Press.

**4** Repeat steps 2 and 3 to add the beige 7½"-wide outer borders.

## FINISHING

**1** Refer to "Completing the Quilt" on page 76 to layer the quilt top, batting, and backing. Quilt as desired.

**2** Sew the beige 2½"-wide binding strips together to form one continuous strip and bind the quilt.

Designed by Kathy Brown; pieced by Pam Vieira-McGinnis; quilted by Carol Hilton

# I was 11 years old

when the game Twister came out. I wanted this game badly, but had been taught never to ask for anything in a store, so that route of acquisition was not to be. Not old enough yet to baby sit, all my extra money came from my allowance, and that was saved for family vacations and newfound Monkees memorabilia. Well, I guess a little birdie whispered in my grandmother's ear, because when Christmas came that year, I received that oh-so-treasured Twister game! I can still remember the excitement and peals of laughter as we played game after game of twisted fun.

The appliquéd circles in this fun-loving quilt remind me of those carefree days playing Twister with my girlfriends. Take a walk in the past with me and create your own version of Twister with this ever-so-easy quilted game.

## MATERIALS

*Yardage is based on 42"-wide fabric.*

¾ yard of red dotted fabric for blocks

¾ yard of red gingham for blocks

¾ yard of blue dotted fabric for blocks

¾ yard of blue strawberry print for blocks

3½ yards of white-dotted tone-on-tone fabric for blocks

⅔ yard of red dotted fabric for inner border

1⅓ yards of blue strawberry print for outer border

⅔ yard of red gingham for binding

5¼ yards of fabric for backing

75" x 93" piece of batting

6 yards of 18"-wide fusible web

## CUTTING

The circle pattern is on page 25. See "Constructing the Blocks" for fusible appliqué instructions before cutting, or use your favorite appliqué method.

From *each* of the ¾-yard pieces, cut:
12 circles

From the white-dotted tone-on-tone fabric, cut:
48 squares, 9½" x 9½"

From the red dotted fabric for inner border, cut:
8 strips, 2½" x 42"

From the blue strawberry print for outer border, cut:
8 strips, 5" x 42"

From the red gingham for binding, cut:
8 strips, 2½" x 42"

## CONSTRUCTING THE BLOCKS

1 Following the manufacturer's instructions, trace the circle pattern onto the paper side of the fusible web. You'll need 48 circles. Cut loosely around the drawn circles and fuse them to the wrong side of the circle fabrics. Cut on the drawn lines to make 48 circles.

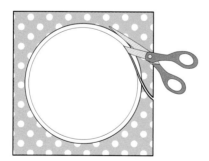

2 Separate the fabrics, stacking all of the same-fabric circles into groups so that you'll have four different groupings: red dotted fabric, red gingham, blue dotted fabric, and blue strawberry-print circles.

3 Fuse the fabric circles onto the 9½" white-dotted tone-on-tone squares, centering the circles within the squares. With coordinating thread, sew a straight stitch around each of the appliquéd circles, approximately ⅛" inside the raw edge of each circle. You can also use a zigzag stitch, blanket stitch, or other decorative stitch on your machine if you prefer.

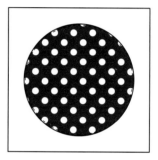

4 Make 12 blocks each of the four fabric combinations.

Make 12 of each.

## ASSEMBLING THE QUILT TOP

1 Using a design wall or other flat surface, arrange the blocks in eight rows of six blocks each as shown.

**②** Sew the blocks into rows. Press seam allowances in opposite directions from row to row. Sew the rows together to form the quilt top.

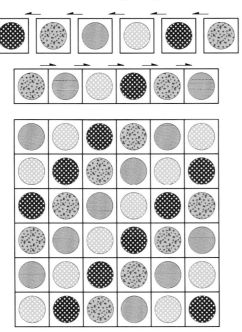

**③** Referring to "Adding Borders" on page 76, sew two red dotted inner-border strips together to make one long strip. Repeat to make four long strips.

**④** Sew the inner borders to the quilt top. Press.

**⑤** Repeat steps 3 and 4 to add the blue strawberry-print outer borders.

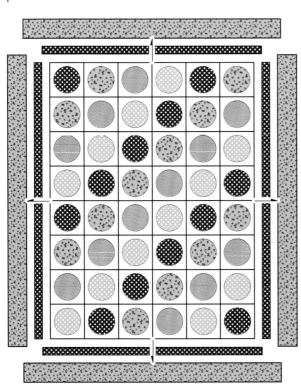

## FINISHING

**①** Refer to "Completing the Quilt" on page 76 to layer the quilt top, batting, and backing. Quilt as desired.

**②** Sew the binding strips together to form one continuous strip and bind the quilt.

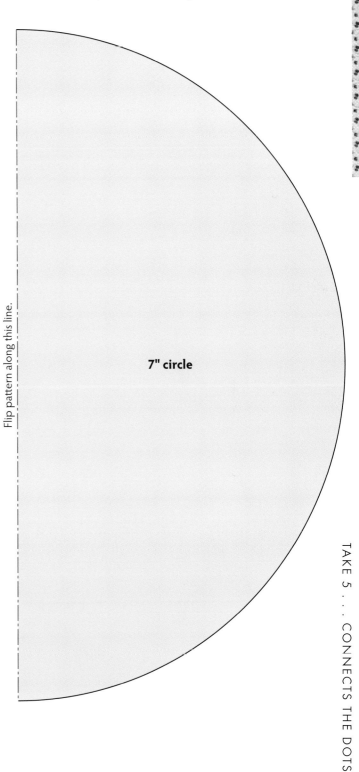

Flip pattern along this line.

7" circle

# take 5...
## SPINS a thread

Designed by Kathy Brown; pieced by Yvonne Smode; quilted by Carol Hilton

# I had the great

fortune when I was growing up of having a mother who was an expert seamstress. No matter what I saw in the Sears, Roebuck and Co. or JCPenney catalog, my mom would find a pattern close to the original. She let me pick out the fabric and went on to make the item seemingly with ease. I loved going into fabric stores—just so that I could go over to the thread cabinets. I was never interested in sewing, so the endless aisles of fabrics held no fascination for me. But the spools of thread—oh my! The rows upon rows of color had my rapt attention. I've always been drawn to color, and these spools were just another vehicle that furthered that interest.

Of course, back then the spools were made of wood. This quilt is a tribute to those wooden spools of thread from my childhood. Perhaps it will spark a warm memory or two for you as well.

## MATERIALS

*Yardage is based on 42"-wide fabric.*

¾ yard of brown floral for blocks

¾ yard of blue print for blocks

¾ yard of brown print for blocks

¾ yard of red print for blocks

2½ yards of muslin for blocks

⅔ yard of blue print for inner border

2½ yards of brown floral for outer border and binding

5 yards of fabric for backing

74" x 86" piece of batting

## CUTTING THE LAYERED PIECES

Refer to "Rotary Cutting" on page 75 to stack the fabrics and straighten the edges. Refer to the cutting diagram below to cut the layered fabrics as indicated, cutting in order from left to right.

**From *each* of the ¾-yard pieces, cut:**

40 rectangles, 2½" x 6½"

20 squares, 2½" x 2½"

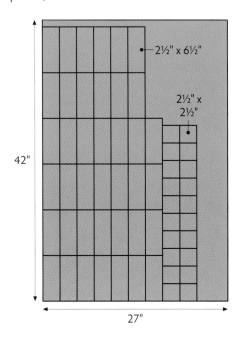

## CUTTING THE REMAINING PIECES

**From the muslin, cut:**

30 strips, 2½" x 42"; crosscut into 480 squares, 2½" x 2½"

**From the blue print for inner border, cut:**

8 strips, 2½" x 42"

**From the brown floral for outer border and binding, cut:**

8 strips, 7½" x 42"

8 strips, 2½" x 42"

## CONSTRUCTING THE BLOCKS

1. Separate the fabrics, stacking all of the same-fabric rectangles and squares into groups so that you'll have five different groupings: brown floral, blue print, brown print, red print, and the muslin squares.

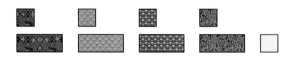

2. Draw a diagonal line from corner to corner on the wrong side of 320 muslin 2½" squares.

3. Place a marked muslin square on the left end of a brown floral 2½" x 6½" rectangle as shown and sew on the drawn line. Repeat on the opposite end of the rectangle. Trim the excess fabric ¼" from the stitched lines. Press. Make 40 of each color combination: brown floral/muslin, blue print/muslin, brown print/muslin, and red print/muslin.

Make 40.

Make 40.   Make 40.   Make 40.

4. Sew muslin 2½" squares to opposite sides of a brown floral 2½" square. Make 20 of each color combination: brown floral/muslin, blue print/muslin, brown print/muslin, and red print/muslin.

5. Sew brown floral units from step 3 to the top and bottom of a blue unit from step 4. Press the seam allowances toward the center.

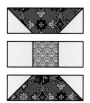

**6** Repeat step 5 to make 20 of each block combination as shown.

Make 20 of each.

## ASSEMBLING THE QUILT TOP

**1** Using a design wall or other flat surface, arrange the completed blocks into 10 rows of eight blocks each, rotating the blocks as shown.

**2** Sew the blocks into rows. Press the seam allowances toward the horizontal Spool blocks. Sew the rows together to form the quilt top. Press the seam allowances in one direction.

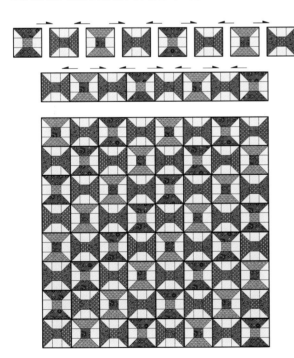

**3** Referring to "Adding Borders" on page 76, sew two blue-print inner-border strips together to make one long strip. Repeat to make four long strips.

**4** Sew the inner borders to the quilt top. Press.

**5** Repeat steps 3 and 4 to add the brown-floral 7½"-wide outer borders.

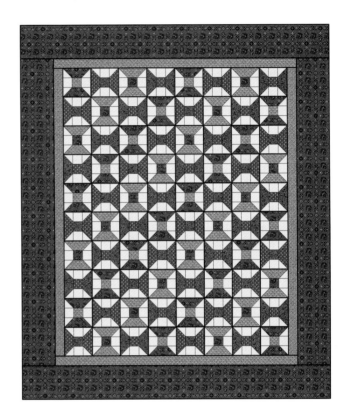

## FINISHING

**1** Refer to "Completing the Quilt" on page 76 to layer the quilt top, batting, and backing. Quilt as desired.

**2** Sew the brown-floral 2½"-wide binding strips together to form one continuous strip and bind the quilt.

# take 5...
# climbs JACOB'S LADDER

Designed by Kathy Brown; pieced by Linda Reed; quilted by Carol Hilton

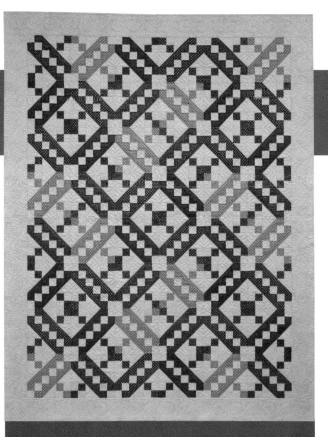

# The neighborhood

I grew up in was the kind of place every kid was happy to call home. With an elementary school, a large park, and a community swimming pool located in the center of our subdivision, it took just a few minutes by bike to meet up with all our friends for a day filled with fun. The park was my favorite place of all to play, with swings that took me to the sky and back, and a whopper of a slide that seemed a hundred feet high. We lined up in droves and climbed step after step after step to reach the towering top of the sturdy steel slide before taking the plunge down the super slick sliding surface!

This quilt, made of Jacob's Ladder blocks, reminds me of that very same slide and the afternoons of fun spent in its open embrace. That wonderful slide stands in its original glory today, still offering rides to all of the children who grace its steps!

## MATERIALS

*Yardage is based on 42"-wide fabric.*

1¼ yards of green print for blocks

1¼ yards of blue print for blocks

1¼ yards of gold print for blocks

1¼ yards of red print for blocks

4¼ yards of muslin for blocks

3¼ yards of muslin for border and binding

8 yards of fabric for backing

92" x 116" piece of batting

## CUTTING THE LAYERED PIECES

Refer to "Rotary Cutting" on page 75 to stack the fabrics and straighten the edges. Refer to the cutting diagram below to cut the layered fabrics as indicated, cutting in order from left to right.

**From *each* of the 1¼-yard pieces, cut:**

8 strips, 2½" x 42"

24 squares, 4⅞" x 4⅞"

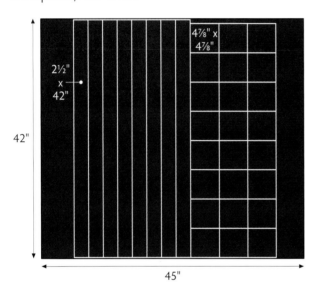

## CUTTING THE REMAINING PIECES

**From the muslin for blocks, cut:**

32 strips, 2½" x 42"

12 strips, 4⅞" x 42"; crosscut into 96 squares, 4⅞" x 4⅞"

**From the muslin for border and binding, cut:**

12 strips, 6½" x 42"

10 strips, 2½" x 42"

## ASSEMBLING THE STRIP SETS

1. Separate the fabrics, stacking all of the same-fabric strips and squares into groups so that you'll have five different groupings: green print, blue print, gold print, red print, and the muslin.

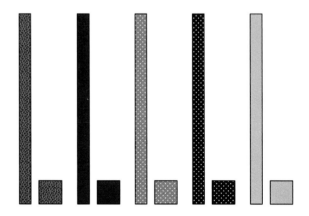

2. Sew a muslin 2½" x 42" strip to each of the green, blue, gold, and red 2½" x 42" strips to make eight strip sets of each color. Press the seam allowances toward the darker strips.

3. From each strip set, cut 15 or 16 segments, 2½" wide, until you have a total of 120 segments of each color.

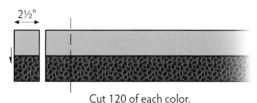

Cut 120 of each color.

4. Stack all of the cut segments into piles, according to color.

## CONSTRUCTING THE BLOCKS

1. Sew two matching strip-set segments together as shown to make a four-patch unit. Repeat to make 60 four-patch units in each color combination.

Make 60 in each color.

2 Draw a diagonal line from corner to corner on the wrong side of each muslin 4⅞" square.

3 Place a marked muslin square right sides together with a colored 4⅞" square. Sew ¼" from each side of the drawn line. Cut on the drawn line to yield two half-square-triangle units. Repeat to make a total of 192 half-square-triangle units.

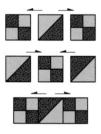

Make 192 total.

4 Arrange five matching four-patch units and four half-square-triangle units of the same color together in rows as shown. Be sure to orient the units correctly. Sew the units together in rows and press. Sew the rows together and press. Make 12 blocks of each color, for a total of 48.

Make 12 of each color.

## ASSEMBLING THE QUILT TOP

1 Using a design wall or other flat surface, arrange the completed blocks in eight rows of six blocks each, rotating the blocks as shown in the quilt layout diagram.

2 Sew the blocks into rows and press the seam allowances in opposite directions from row to row. Sew the rows together to make the quilt top.

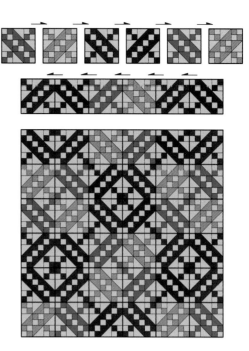

3 Referring to "Adding Borders" on page 76, sew three muslin 6½"-wide border strips together to make one long strip. Repeat to make four long strips.

4 Sew the borders to the quilt top. Press.

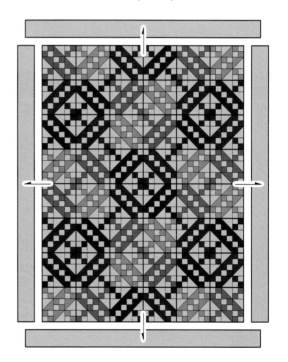

## FINISHING

1 Refer to "Completing the Quilt" on page 76 to layer the quilt top, batting, and backing. Quilt as desired.

2 Sew the muslin 2½"-wide binding strips together to form one continuous strip and bind the quilt.

# take 5 . . .

# spins a TALL TALE

Designed by Kathy Brown; pieced by Andrea Keith; quilted by Carol Hilton

# As a youngster,

I was known to tell a tall tale every now and then for reasons that I thought were important at the time. And, as life would have it, most of those tall tales eventually caught up with me in one way or another. Or before they did, I'd fess up.

So here I am, fessing up again. "Take 5 Spins a Tall Tale" doesn't use five fabrics. It uses five fabrics, plus a neutral. Whew! I feel so much better now! I'm ready—are you? Let's start making this fantastic Take 5 (ahem, Take 6) quilt!

## MATERIALS

*Yardage is based on 42"-wide fabric.*

½ yard of dark-brown floral for blocks

½ yard of red dotted print for blocks

½ yard of light-brown floral for blocks

½ yard of red leaf print for blocks

⅝ yard of cream solid for blocks

1¾ yards of cream floral for blocks

⅔ yard of red dotted print for inner border

2¼ yards of dark-brown floral for outer border and binding

5 yards of fabric for backing

72" x 84" piece of batting

## CUTTING THE LAYERED PIECES

Refer to "Rotary Cutting" on page 75 to stack the fabrics and straighten the edges. Refer to the cutting diagram below to cut the layered fabrics as indicated, cutting in order from left to right.

**From *each* of the ½-yard pieces, cut:**

10 squares, 6⅞" x 6⅞"

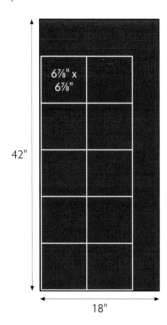

## CUTTING THE REMAINING PIECES

**From the cream floral, cut:**

8 strips, 6⅞" x 42"; crosscut into 40 squares, 6⅞" x 6⅞"

**From the cream solid, cut:**

8 strips, 2" x 42"; crosscut into 160 squares, 2" x 2"

**From the red dotted print for inner border, cut:**

8 strips, 2½" x 42"

**From the dark-brown floral for outer border and binding, cut:**

8 strips, 6½" x 42"

8 strips, 2½" x 42"

## CONSTRUCTING THE BLOCKS

❶ Separate the fabrics, stacking all of the same-fabric squares into groups so that you'll have six different groupings: dark-brown floral, red dotted print, light-brown floral, red leaf print, cream floral, and cream solid.

❷ Draw a diagonal line from corner to corner on the wrong side of the 40 cream-floral 6⅞" squares.

❸ Place a marked cream-floral square right sides together with a colored 6⅞" square. Sew ¼" from both sides of the drawn line. Cut on the drawn line to yield two half-square-triangle units. Make a total of 80 units.

Make 80 total.

❹ Draw a diagonal line from corner to corner on the wrong side of the 160 cream-solid 2" squares.

❺ Position a marked cream square right sides together on one corner of a half-square-triangle unit, over the seam where the two fabrics are joined. The drawn line should be perpendicular to the seam line of the half-square-triangle unit. Sew on the drawn line. Trim the excess fabric ¼" from the sewn line and press the triangle outward. Repeat on the opposite corner. Do this for each half-square-triangle unit.

**6** Sew four matching units from step 5 together, orienting them as shown to make a block.

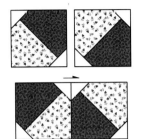 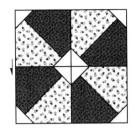 

**7** Repeat step 6 to make five blocks of each print.

## ASSEMBLING THE QUILT TOP

**1** Using a design wall or other flat surface, arrange the completed blocks in five rows of four blocks each as shown.

**2** Sew the blocks into rows, pressing the seam allowances in opposite directions from row to row. Sew the rows together to form the quilt top. Press the seam allowances in one direction.

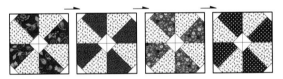

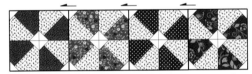

**3** Referring to "Adding Borders" on page 76, sew two red dotted inner-border strips together to make one long strip. Repeat to make four long strips.

**4** Sew the inner borders to the quilt top. Press.

**5** Repeat steps 3 and 4 to add the dark-brown floral 6½"-wide outer borders.

## FINISHING

**1** Refer to "Completing the Quilt" on page 76 to layer the quilt top, batting, and backing. Quilt as desired.

**2** Sew the dark-brown floral 2½"-wide binding strips together to form one continuous strip and bind the quilt.

Designed by Kathy Brown; pieced by Denise Bayer; quilted by Carol Hilton

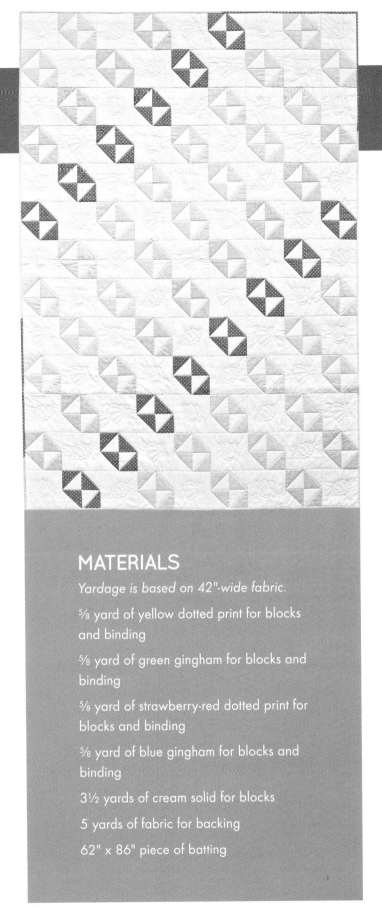

**Finished Quilt:** 54" x 78" — **Finished Block:** 6" x 6"

My dad's father grew up in the coastal town of Ogunquit, Maine. A music professor by trade, he spent many years teaching piano at Louisiana State University. Grammie and Gramps never lost their love for coastal Maine, however, and kept a summer home there. Every summer when I was young, they would travel back to Maine and spend time in the cooler weather. Upon returning to Louisiana, they'd greet us with special treats from Maine. Among my favorites were maple sugar blocks that seemed to melt in my mouth the moment they landed on my tongue! A beautiful box of seashells collected on my grandmother's early morning walks still sits in my studio today. One summer, to my delight, I opened my present and found a box of beautiful candies—softly colored pastels wrapped in waxed-paper twists. For a southern-Louisiana girl, this was a newfound treasure—saltwater taffy!

This quilt brings memories of that box of saltwater taffy right back to me. The soothing creaminess of the simple squares next to the bright and pastel taffy blocks sets the tone for a very special memory quilt!

## MATERIALS

*Yardage is based on 42"-wide fabric.*

⅝ yard of yellow dotted print for blocks and binding

⅝ yard of green gingham for blocks and binding

⅝ yard of strawberry-red dotted print for blocks and binding

⅝ yard of blue gingham for blocks and binding

3½ yards of cream solid for blocks

5 yards of fabric for backing

62" x 86" piece of batting

## CUTTING THE LAYERED PIECES

Refer to "Rotary Cutting" on page 75 to stack the fabrics and straighten the edges. Refer to the cutting diagram below to cut the layered fabrics as indicated, cutting in order from left to right. There will be two extra red and two extra blue squares left over. Put these in your stash for future use.

**From *each* of the ⅝-yard pieces, cut:**
30 squares, 3⅞" x 3⅞"

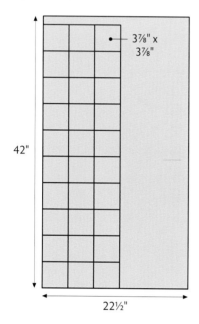

## CUTTING THE REMAINING PIECES

**From the cream solid, cut:**

12 strips, 3⅞" x 42"; crosscut into 116 squares, 3⅞" x 3⅞"

10 strips, 6½" x 42"; crosscut into 59 squares, 6½" x 6½"

**From the 4 leftover prints for blocks, cut a *total* of:**
7 binding strips, 2½" x 42"

## CONSTRUCTING THE BLOCKS

1. Separate the fabrics, stacking all of the same-fabric squares into groups so that you'll have six different groupings: yellow dotted print, green gingham, strawberry-red dotted print, blue gingham, small cream solid, and large cream solid.

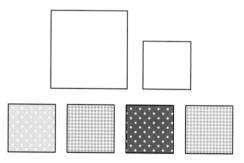

2. Draw a diagonal line from corner to corner on the wrong side of the 116 cream-solid 3⅞" squares. Place a cream-solid square right sides together with a colored 3⅞" square. Sew ¼" from both sides of the drawn line. Cut on the drawn line to yield two half-square-triangle units. Make 232.

Make 232 total.

3. Sew four matching half-square-triangle units together as shown, making certain to orient the units correctly.

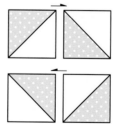 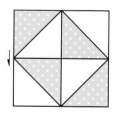

4. Repeat with the remaining half-square-triangle units to make a total of 58 blocks.

## ASSEMBLING THE QUILT TOP

1. Using a design wall or other flat surface, arrange the completed blocks and cream-solid squares into 13 rows of nine blocks each, alternating the blocks as shown.

2. Sew the blocks into rows, pressing the seam allowances toward the cream-solid squares. Sew the rows together and press the seam allowances in one direction.

## FINISHING

1. Refer to "Completing the Quilt" on page 76 to layer the quilt top, batting, and backing. Quilt as desired.

2. Sew the binding strips together to form one continuous strip and bind the quilt.

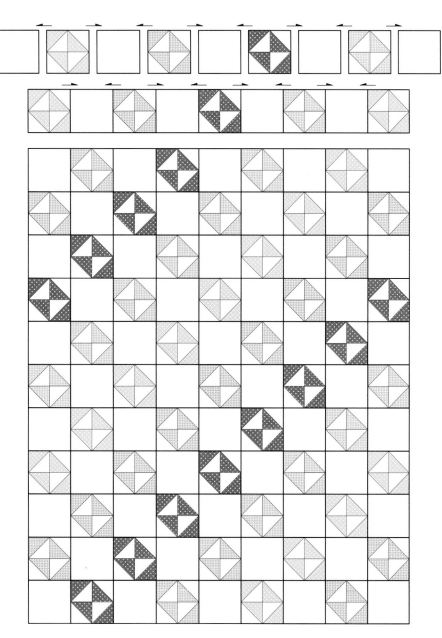

Designed by Kathy Brown; pieced by Linda Reed; quilted by Carol Hilton

# Louisiana is home

to many beautiful and historic plantation estates, a number of which have been used as filming locations by the motion-picture industry. One of those homes, Ashland-Belle Helene, was used in the 1957 movie *Band of Angels*, starring Clark Gable and Yvonne De Carlo. My great-aunt and great-uncle lived next door to the plantation, and on several occasions had Clark Gable over to their home for one of my aunt's home-cooked country breakfasts. On one of those mornings, my mom bundled up my brother and me and drove us down to enjoy one of those special breakfasts! As the family story goes, Clark Gable took one look at this tiny little infant (me!) and promptly sat down in a rocking chair and fed me my bottle! Ever since then, it's said that I can be found in a rocking chair wherever I go.

This star-studded quilt evokes memories of that story told over and over again at family get-togethers.

## MATERIALS

*Yardage is based on 42"-wide fabric.*

½ yard of red dotted print for blocks

½ yard of purple dotted print for blocks

½ yard of gold dotted print for blocks

1⅓ yards of black floral for blocks

2⅝ yards of cream swirl print for blocks

⅔ yard of cream swirl print for inner border

2¼ yards of black floral for outer border and binding

5⅓ yards of fabric for backing

72" x 96" piece of batting

## CUTTING THE LAYERED FABRICS

Refer to "Rotary Cutting" on page 75 to stack the cuts of fabrics and straighten the edges. Refer to the cutting diagram below to cut the layered fabrics as indicated, cutting in order from left to right.

**From *each* of the ½-yard pieces, cut:**

16 rectangles, 3½" x 6½"

8 squares, 3⅞" x 3⅞"

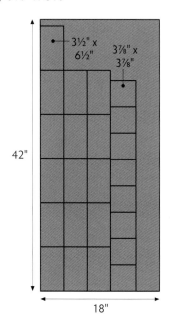

## CUTTING THE REMAINING PIECES

**From the black floral for blocks, cut:**

3 strips, 3⅞" x 42"; crosscut into 24 squares, 3⅞" x 3⅞"

8 strips, 3½" x 42"; crosscut into 48 rectangles, 3½" x 6½"

**From the cream swirl print for blocks, cut:**

5 strips, 3⅞" x 42"; crosscut into 48 squares, 3⅞" x 3⅞"

18 strips, 3½" x 42"; crosscut into 192 squares, 3½" x 3½"

**From the cream swirl print for inner border, cut:**

8 strips, 2½" x 42"

**From the black floral for outer border and binding, cut:**

8 strips, 6½" x 42"

8 strips, 2½" x 42"

## CONSTRUCTING THE BLOCKS

① Separate the fabrics, stacking all of the same-fabric squares and rectangles into groups so that you'll have 10 different groupings: red dotted squares, red dotted rectangles, purple dotted squares, purple dotted rectangles, gold dotted squares, gold dotted rectangles, black floral squares, black floral rectangles, and large and small cream-swirl squares.

② Draw a diagonal line from corner to corner on the wrong side of the cream-swirl 3⅞" squares and 96 of the cream-swirl 3½" squares.

③ Place a marked cream-swirl 3⅞" square right sides together with a colored 3⅞" square. Keeping right sides together, sew ¼" from both sides of the drawn line. Cut on the drawn line to yield two half-square-triangle units. Repeat to make a total of 96 (16 each of red dotted, purple dotted, and gold dotted fabrics and 48 of black floral).

Make 96 total.

④ Place a marked cream-swirl 3½" square right sides together with a colored 3½" x 6½" rectangle so that the line is angled in the direction shown. Sew on the drawn line. Trim the excess fabric ¼" from the sewn line, fold back the triangle, and press. Make a total of 96 as shown.

Make 16.

Make 16.     Make 16.     Make 48.

**5** Sew a half-square-triangle unit to a cream-swirl square, orienting the pieces as shown.

Make 16.     Make 16.     Make 16.     Make 48.

**6** Sew each unit from step 5 to the right side of a unit from step 4 as shown.

Make 16.     Make 16.     Make 16.

Make 16.     Make 16.     Make 16.

**7** Arrange and sew four matching units together, orienting them as shown to make a block. Make four of each as shown

Make 4 of each.

# ASSEMBLING THE QUILT TOP

**1** Using a design wall or other flat surface, arrange the completed blocks in six rows of four blocks each as shown in the quilt layout diagram.

**2** Sew the blocks into rows and press the seam allowances in opposite directions from row to row. Sew the rows together and press the seam allowances in one direction.

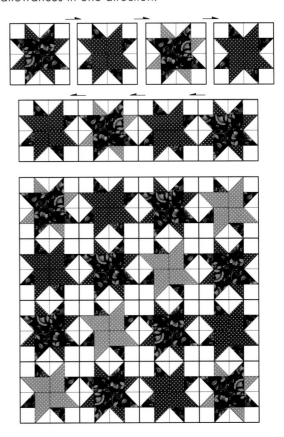

**3** Referring to "Adding Borders" on page 76, sew two cream-swirl inner-border strips together to make one long strip. Repeat to make four long strips.

**4** Sew the inner borders to the quilt top. Press.

**5** Repeat steps 3 and 4 to add the black floral 6½"-wide outer borders.

# FINISHING

**1** Refer to "Completing the Quilt" on page 76 to layer the quilt top, batting, and backing. Quilt as desired.

**2** Sew the black floral 2½"-wide binding strips together to form one continuous strip and bind the quilt.

# take ⑤...
# TIMES 2

Designed, pieced, and quilted by Kathy Brown

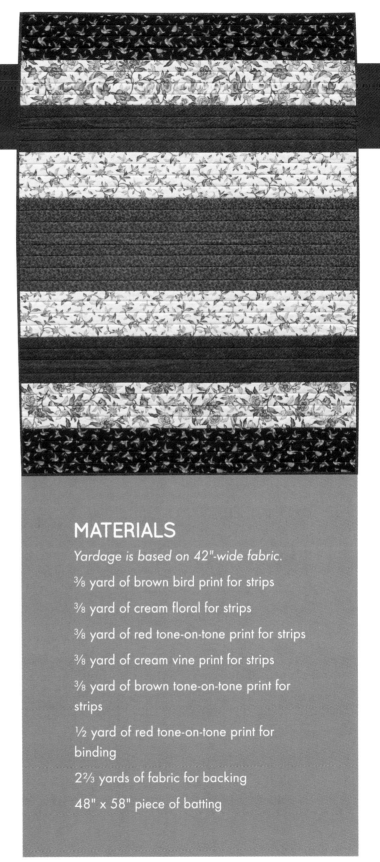

**Finished Quilt:** 40" x 50"

# About a year into

my quilting journey I discovered the quilt-as-you-go technique and fell in love with it. The thought of being able to make a quilt top and have it quilted and finished in one swift effort was just incredible to me. With this fun quilt, we're going to marry the Take 5 technique with the quilt-as-you-go technique! You'll be so amazed at the speed with which you can make this fun, fast, and fabulous strip quilt. Perfect for a crib quilt, a child's blankie, or just a quick lap quilt for your hearth and home, you'll want to make this winning Take 5 quilt again and again.

This quilt is a perfect candidate for using many of those beautiful fabrics that you hate to cut up into small pieces.

## MATERIALS

*Yardage is based on 42"-wide fabric.*

⅜ yard of brown bird print for strips

⅜ yard of cream floral for strips

⅜ yard of red tone-on-tone print for strips

⅜ yard of cream vine print for strips

⅜ yard of brown tone-on-tone print for strips

½ yard of red tone-on-tone print for binding

2⅔ yards of fabric for backing

48" x 58" piece of batting

## CUTTING THE LAYERED PIECES

Refer to "Rotary Cutting" on page 75 to stack the fabrics and straighten the edges. Refer to the cutting diagram below to cut the layered fabrics as indicated.

**From *each* of the ⅜-yard pieces, cut:**
2 strips, 5½" x 42"

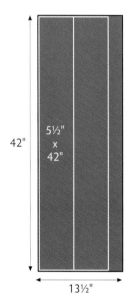

## CUTTING THE REMAINING PIECES

**From the red tone-on-tone print for binding, cut:**
6 strips, 2½" x 42"

## CONSTRUCTING AND QUILTING THE QUILT

❶ Separate the fabrics, stacking all of the same-fabric strips into groups so that you have five different groupings: brown bird print, cream floral, red tone-on-tone print, cream vine print, and brown tone-on-tone print.

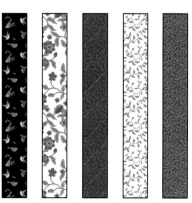

❷ Using a design wall or other flat surface, arrange the strips as shown.

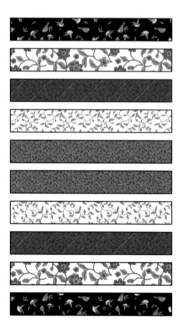

❸ Sew the two brown tone-on-tone strips together along the length of the strips. Press the seam allowances open, not to the side.

❹ Place the backing fabric right side down on a flat surface. Place the batting on top of the backing, smoothing out any wrinkles.

❺ Place the sewn strips from step 3 right sides up in the center of the backing and batting layers. Use quilters' pins to pin along each side and down the seam to hold the three layers together.

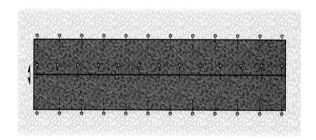

**6** Stitch a straight line ½" from both sides of the pinned seam using thread in a coordinating color. Continue sewing straight lines at 1" intervals until you reach the edge of the strip. Remove all pins.

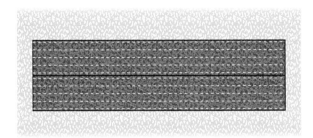

**7** Place a cream vine-print strip right side down on top of one of the brown tone-on-tone strips, aligning the raw edges. Pin to hold in place. Stitch the cream vine-print strip to the brown tone-on-tone strip, ¼" from the raw edge.

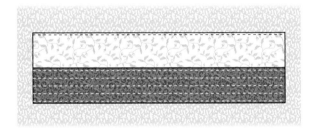

**8** Remove pins and fold the cream vine strip right side up. Re-pin to keep the strip straight and in place. Stitch straight lines along the length of the cream vine-print strip as you did before.

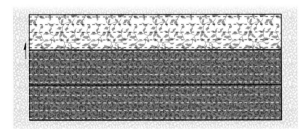

**9** Repeat steps 7 and 8 with a second cream vine-print strip on the opposite side of the brown strips. Repeat the process to add the remaining strips to alternate sides until all strips have been sewn and quilted.

**10** Trim the excess batting and backing fabric, and square up the quilt so that it measures 40½" x 50½".

## FINISHING

Refer to "Binding" on page 77. Sew the binding strips together to form one continuous strip and bind the quilt.

Designed by Kathy Brown; pieced by Janell Crosslin; quilted by Carol Hilton

**Finished Quilt:** 63½" x 79½"
**Finished Block:** 2½" and 4½" x 4½"

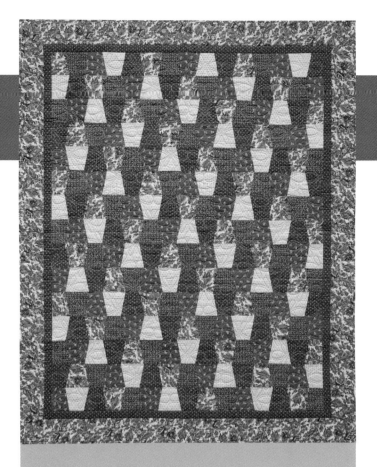

## When my two

brothers and I were very young, we lived next door to a family with four boys, across the street from a family with six boys, and catty-corner from a family with three boys. It was inevitable that I grew up as a certified tomboy—a bike-riding, football-playing, tree-climbing, ditch-jumping, box-hockey champ of a tomboy! I was as rough and tumble as any of my cohorts for most of my youth—much to my mom's chagrin. As the years passed, I slowly eased up on my tomboy ways, and my mom finally had a daughter—even if that daughter came complete with quite a few battle scars.

The Tumbler block in this quilt reminds me of all those fun-filled tomboy days and mingles them with the more feminine traits that I finally picked up along the way!

## MATERIALS

*Yardage is based on 42"-wide fabric.*

1 yard of tan floral for blocks

1 yard of blue floral for blocks

1 yard of brown floral for blocks

1 yard of cream print for blocks

1 yard of red print for blocks

⅝ yard of red print for inner border

2 yards of tan floral for outer border and binding

5 yards of fabric for backing

72" x 88" piece of batting

## CUTTING THE LAYERED PIECES

Refer to "Rotary Cutting" on page 75 to stack the fabrics and straighten the edges. Refer to the cutting diagram below to cut the layered fabrics as indicated, cutting in order from left to right.

**From *each* of the 1-yard pieces, cut:**

45 squares, 5" x 5"

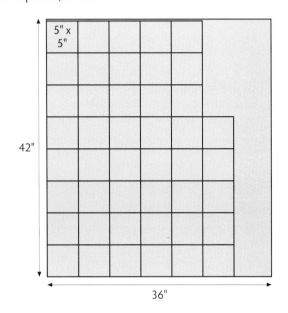

## CUTTING THE REMAINING PIECES

**From the red print for inner border, cut:**

8 strips, 2" x 42"

**From the tan floral for outer border and binding, cut:**

8 strips, 5" x 42"

8 strips, 2½" x 42"

## ORGANIZING AND CUTTING THE BLOCKS

1. Separate the fabrics, stacking all of the same-fabric squares into groups so that you'll have five different groupings: tan floral, blue floral, brown floral, cream print, and red print.

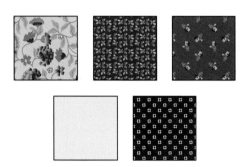

2. Stack five same-fabric squares on a cutting mat, right side up, making sure that nothing shows but the top square. (The pile is straight and square!) Mark a point on the top square, 1" in from the left side, and mark a second point 1" in from the right side. Draw a line from the bottom-left corner of the top square to the left marked point, and from the bottom-right corner of the top square to the right marked point.

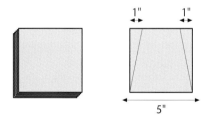

3. Make sure the pile is still straight and square. Using a rotary cutter and ruler, cut through the pile along the two marked lines. Remove the excess and discard.

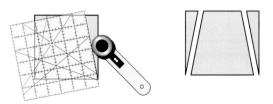

Repeat steps 2 and 3 to cut the remaining squares in each pile.

## ASSEMBLING THE QUILT TOP

**1** Using a design wall or other flat surface, arrange the Tumbler blocks in 15 rows of 15 blocks each as shown in the quilt layout diagram. Keep the fabric colors in the same sequence in each row, and begin each row with the next to the last fabric from the previous row. I suggest sewing the rows together in three sections of five rows each.

**2** Sew the blocks together into rows by placing the pieces right sides together, offsetting the corners. You may want to pin the pieces to ensure an accurate match. Press the seam allowances in opposite directions from row to row.

 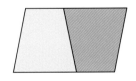

**3** Sew the rows together to form the quilt top.

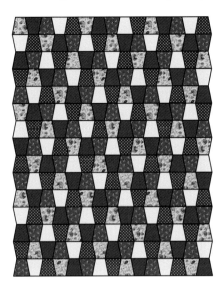

**4** Trim the quilt top on the left and right sides. Make sure the corners are square.

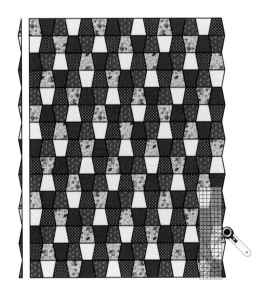

**5** Referring to "Adding Borders" on page 76 sew two red-print inner-border strips together to make one long strip. Repeat to make four long strips.

**6** Sew the inner borders to the quilt top. Press.

**7** Repeat steps 5 and 6 to add the tan floral 5"-wide outer borders.

## FINISHING

**1** Refer to "Completing the Quilt" on page 76 to layer the quilt top, batting, and backing. Quilt as desired.

**2** Sew the tan floral 2½"-wide binding strips together to form one continuous strip and bind the quilt.

# take 5 ... flies a KITE

Designed by Kathy Brown; pieced by Wanda Hoffman; quilted by Carol Hilton

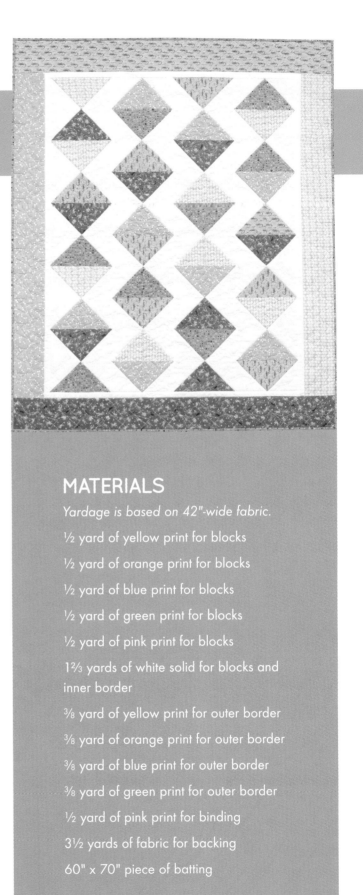

# One bright spring day

when my daughter was about three years old, we packed a picnic basket and headed to the park for a wonderful family day. The weather was crisp and cool, there wasn't a cloud in the sky, and the winds were just right for flying a kite. We spread a quilt on the ground, and my husband and daughter put their heads together as they worked to assemble her first kite—a Sesame Street special. The winds picked up, the excitement built, and the kite took flight—higher and higher it flew, just dancing in the wind. The higher it flew, the more worried our daughter became. And then it happened. The buckets of tears started flowing, and in between sobs we found out that she just couldn't bear to see Bert and Ernie fly away. They might never come back! A few minutes of reeling in the line reassured her that her favorite characters were still close by, and the remainder of the day was saved.

The diamond-shaped blocks in this quilt look a bit like kites floating in the air. Isn't there a special little girl or boy you'd like to make a kite quilt for? This one will surely steal their hearts.

## MATERIALS

*Yardage is based on 42"-wide fabric.*

½ yard of yellow print for blocks

½ yard of orange print for blocks

½ yard of blue print for blocks

½ yard of green print for blocks

½ yard of pink print for blocks

1⅔ yards of white solid for blocks and inner border

⅜ yard of yellow print for outer border

⅜ yard of orange print for outer border

⅜ yard of blue print for outer border

⅜ yard of green print for outer border

½ yard of pink print for binding

3½ yards of fabric for backing

60" x 70" piece of batting

## CUTTING THE LAYERED PIECES

Refer to "Rotary Cutting" on page 75 to stack the fabrics and straighten the edges. Refer to the cutting diagram below to cut the layered fabrics as indicated, cutting in order from left to right.

From *each* of the ½-yard pieces for blocks, cut:

8 squares, 5⅞" x 5⅞"

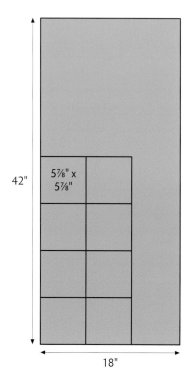

## CUTTING THE REMAINING PIECES

From the white solid for blocks and inner border, cut:

7 strips, 5⅞" x 42"; crosscut into 40 squares, 5⅞" x 5⅞"

8 strips, 1½" x 42"

From *each* of the 4 outer-border fabrics, cut:

2 strips, 5½" x 42"

From the binding fabric, cut:

6 strips, 2½" x 42"

## CONSTRUCTING THE BLOCKS

1. Separate the fabrics, stacking all of the same-fabric squares into piles so that you'll have six different groupings: yellow, orange, blue, green, and pink prints, and white solid.

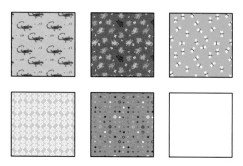

2. Draw a diagonal line from corner to corner on the wrong side of the white 5⅞" squares.

3. Place a marked white square right sides together with a colored 5⅞" square. Sew ¼" from both sides of the drawn line. Cut on the drawn line to yield two half-square-triangle units. Repeat to make 80.

Make 80 total.

4. Sew two matching half-square-triangle units together, orienting them as shown to make the block. Make 40 blocks.

  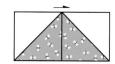

Make 40.

## ASSEMBLING THE QUILT TOP

1. Using a design wall or other flat surface, arrange the completed blocks in 10 rows of four blocks each as shown in the quilt layout diagram.

2. Sew the blocks into rows, pressing the seam allowances in opposite directions from row to row. Sew the rows together and press.

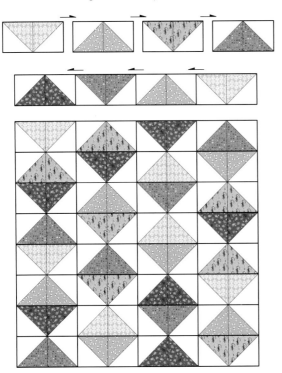

3. Referring to "Adding Borders" on page 76, sew two white inner-border strips together to make one long strip. Repeat to make four long strips.

4. Sew the inner borders to the quilt top. Press.

5. Sew the 5½" x 42" strips together in matching pairs and add the outer borders.

## FINISHING

1. Refer to "Completing the Quilt" on page 76 to layer the quilt top, batting, and backing. Quilt as desired.

2. Sew the binding strips together to form one continuous strip and bind the quilt.

# take ⑤ . . .
# gets a BUZZ cut

Designed by Kathy Brown; pieced by Cheryl Wilks; quilted by Carol Hilton

# When I was a child,

the end of every school year signaled the beginning of summer fun: swimming, sleepovers, playing at the park, riding bikes till the street lights came on at night, and buzz cuts. On the first day of summer, Mom would put my two brothers and me in the car and head to the local barbershop. There, armed with a set of clippers as loud as a buzz saw, the barber would proceed to shear off my brothers' hair until there was nothing left but the smile on their faces!

They were as happy as two young boys could be, armed with the fact that they would be so much cooler in the sweltering Louisiana summer, and there would be no more barbershop visits until the beginning of the next school year! Summer had indeed arrived!

## MATERIALS

*Yardage is based on 42"-wide fabric.*

⅝ yard of dark-brown floral for blocks

⅝ yard of cream floral for blocks

⅝ yard of light-brown floral for blocks

⅝ yard of olive-green print for blocks

⅝ yard of gold print for blocks

2¾ yard of tan solid for blocks

⅔ yard of olive-green print for inner border

2⅓ yards of dark-brown floral for outer border and binding

7 yards of fabric for backing

84" x 96" piece of batting

## CUTTING THE LAYERED FABRICS

Refer to "Rotary Cutting" on page 75 to stack the fabrics and straighten the edges. Refer to the cutting diagram below to cut the layered fabrics as indicated, cutting in order from left to right.

**From *each* of the ⅝-yard pieces, cut:**

24 rectangles, 2½" x 4½"

24 rectangles, 2½" x 6½"

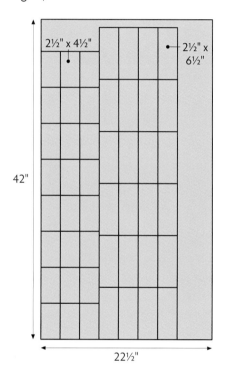

## CUTTING THE REMAINING PIECES

**From the tan solid for blocks, cut:**

35 strips, 2½" x 42"; crosscut into:

 120 rectangles, 2½" x 6½"

 120 rectangles, 2½" x 4½"

**From the olive-green print for inner border, cut:**

8 strips, 2½" x 42"

**From the dark-brown floral for outer border and binding, cut:**

8 strips, 6½" x 42"

9 strips, 2½" x 42"

## CONSTRUCTING THE BLOCKS

1 Separate the fabrics, stacking all of the same-fabric strips into groups so that you have six different groupings: dark-brown floral, cream floral, light-brown floral, olive-green print, gold print, and tan solid.

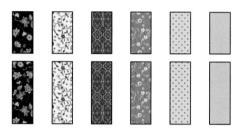

2 Sew a print 2½" x 4½" rectangle and a tan-solid 2½" x 4½" rectangle together diagonally as shown to make a pieced rectangle. Trim the excess, leaving a ¼" seam allowance and press. Using all of the 4½" rectangles, make 120 pieced rectangles.

Make 120.

3 Sew a pieced rectangle between a matching print 2½" x 6½" rectangle and a tan-solid rectangle, orienting the pieced rectangle as shown. Make four units.

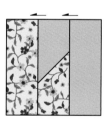

Make 4.

**4** Arrange the four units, orienting them as shown, and sew them together in rows. Sew the rows together to make a block.

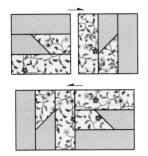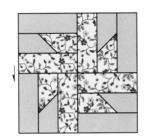

**5** Repeat steps 3 and 4 to complete 30 blocks.

## ASSEMBLING THE QUILT TOP

**1** Using a design wall or other flat surface, arrange the completed blocks in six rows of five blocks each as shown in the quilt layout diagram.

**2** Sew the blocks into rows, pressing the seam allowances in opposite directions from row to row. Sew the rows together to form the quilt top. Press.

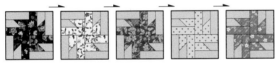

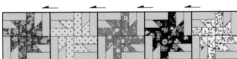

**3** Referring to "Adding Borders" on page 76, sew two olive-green inner-border strips together to make one long strip. Repeat to make four long strips.

**4** Sew the inner borders to the quilt top. Press.

**5** Repeat steps 3 and 4 to add the dark-brown floral 6½"-wide outer borders.

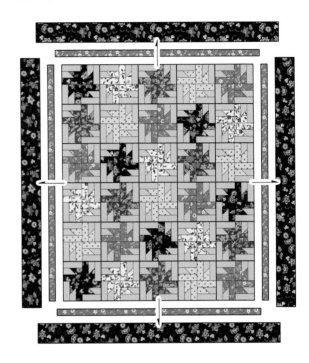

## FINISHING

**1** Refer to "Completing the Quilt" on page 76 to layer the quilt top, batting, and backing. Quilt as desired.

**2** Sew the dark-brown floral 2½"-wide binding strips together to form one continuous strip and bind the quilt.

Designed by Kathy Brown; pieced by Linda Reed; quilted by Carol Hilton

**Finished Quilt:** 61" x 73" — **Finished Block:** 6" x 6"

I was always scared

of the dark when I was a child. I never knew what was hiding in the shadows just waiting to jump out and frighten me! My mom tried in vain to help me get over this fear by assigning a new chore for me to do every night. It was my job to go around the house and close the drapes—but she stipulated that I could only do this after it turned dark every night. Needless to say, I had to devise a way to get this done! So, I would slink up to a window, reach my hand up, and yank on the drapery cord till the drapes closed, then casually stand up and stroll out of the room acting like everything was normal. Did my "chore" cure me? No. Was I terrified every night? Yes! But—as it is with most childhood fears—this apprehension went away on its own, thank goodness!

The way the light fabrics "hide" behind the dark fabrics in this quilt reminds me of those many nights spent sneaking up to the windows of my house, and I smile with the silliness of it all!

## MATERIALS

*Yardage is based on 42"-wide fabric.*

½ yard of pink floral for blocks

½ yard of blue toile for blocks

½ yard of cream vine print for blocks

½ yard of pink toile for blocks

1¾ yards of black floral for blocks

½ yard of blue toile for inner border

2⅛ yards of black floral for outer border and binding

4½ yards of fabric for backing

69" x 81" piece of batting

## CUTTING THE LAYERED PIECES

Refer to "Rotary Cutting" on page 75 to stack the fabrics and straighten the edges. Refer to the cutting diagram below to cut the layered fabrics as indicated, cutting in order from left to right.

From *each* of the ½-yard pieces for blocks, cut:
10 squares, 6⅞" x 6⅞"

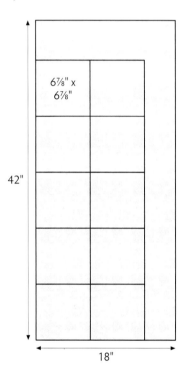

## CUTTING THE REMAINING PIECES

From the black floral for blocks, cut:
8 strips, 6⅞" x 42"; crosscut into 40 squares, 6⅞" x 6⅞"

From the blue toile for inner border, cut:
8 strips, 1" x 42"

From the black floral for outer border and binding, cut:
8 strips, 6½" x 42"
7 strips, 2½" x 42"

## CONSTRUCTING THE BLOCKS

1. Separate the fabrics, stacking all of the same-fabric squares into piles so that you'll have five different groupings: pink floral, blue toile, cream vine print, pink toile, and black floral.

2. Draw a diagonal line from corner to corner on the wrong side of each black floral 6⅞" square with a light chalk pencil or similar marker.

3. Place a marked black floral square right sides together with a print 6⅞" square. Sew ¼" from both sides of the drawn line. Cut on the drawn line to yield two half-square-triangle blocks. Make 80 blocks.

Make 80 total.

## ASSEMBLING THE QUILT TOP

1. Using a design wall or other flat surface, arrange the completed blocks in 10 rows of eight blocks each, orienting the blocks as shown.

2. Sew the blocks into rows, pressing the seam allowances in opposite directions from row to row. Sew the rows together and press.

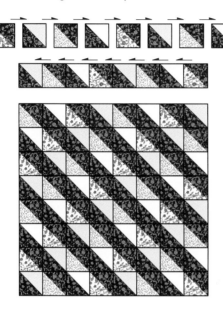

3. Referring to "Adding Borders" on page 76, sew two blue toile inner-border strips together to make one long strip. Repeat to make four long strips.

4. Sew the inner borders to the quilt top. Press.

5. Repeat steps 3 and 4 to add the black floral 6½"-wide outer borders.

## FINISHING

1. Refer to "Completing the Quilt" on page 76 to layer the quilt top, batting, and backing. Quilt as desired.

2. Sew the black floral 2½"-wide binding strips together to form one continuous strip and bind the quilt.

Designed by Kathy Brown; pieced by Linda Reed; quilted by Carol Hilton

**Finished Quilt:** 64" x 80" — **Finished Block:** 16" x 16"

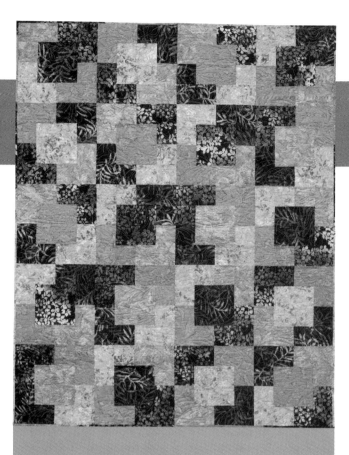

# I grew up in the

1950s and '60s when drugstores were, for the most part, individually owned. Our local drugstore was stocked with everything you could possibly need, including an old-fashioned soda fountain serving fabulous milkshakes and the best hamburgers anyone could sink their teeth into.

One hot summer afternoon, my mom put us in the car for a short drive to Dearman's Drug Store. What we thought was to be a trip to pick up a few items that mom needed turned out to be an excuse to get three cranky kids out of the hot summer sun and into the cool confines of the drugstore for a scoop of ice cream. To our delight, not only did the soda jerk offer the usual chocolate, vanilla, and strawberry flavors, but she also brought out a new delicacy—spumoni! Intrigued by the minty green, chocolate brown, and icy pink colors all swirled together, we each ordered a scoop of this wonderful new concoction!

Whenever I see these same colors combined, I think back to that hot summer day. This quilt would make the perfect accompaniment to a big bowl of spumoni!

## MATERIALS

*Yardage is based on 42"-wide fabric.*

1½ yards of black leaf-print batik for blocks and binding

1½ yards of black floral batik for blocks and binding

1½ yards of gold tone-on-tone batik for blocks and binding

1½ yards of pink tone-on-tone batik for blocks and binding

1½ yards of green leaf batik for blocks and binding

5 yards of fabric for backing

72" x 88" piece of batting

## CUTTING THE LAYERED PIECES

Refer to "Rotary Cutting" on page 75 to stack the fabrics and straighten the edges. Refer to the cutting diagram below to cut the layered fabrics as indicated, cutting in order from left to right.

**From *each* of the batik 1½-yard pieces, cut:**

4 squares, 8½" x 8½"

16 rectangles, 4½" x 8½"

16 squares, 4½" x 4½"

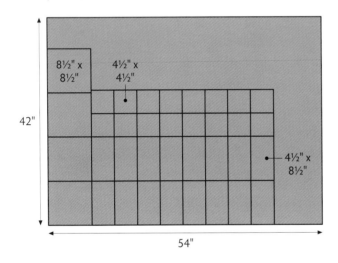

## CUTTING THE BINDING

**From *each* of the remaining block fabrics, cut:**

5 strips, 2½" x 15"

## CONSTRUCTING THE BLOCKS

1. Separate the fabrics, stacking all of the same-fabric squares and rectangles into groups so that you'll have five groupings: black leaf-print batik, black floral batik, gold tone-on-tone batik, green leaf batik, and pink tone-on-tone batik.

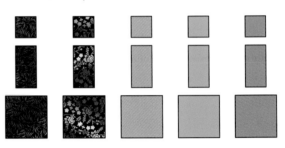

2. Select one 8½" square for the first block. Then choose one 4½" x 8½" rectangle and one 4½" square of each of the other four fabrics to make one block.

3. Sew the 4½" x 8½" rectangles together in pairs along the short ends and sew the 4½" squares together in pairs.

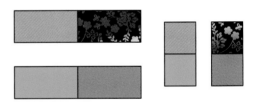

4. Sew the pieced squares to the sides of the center square, and then sew the rectangles to the top and bottom.

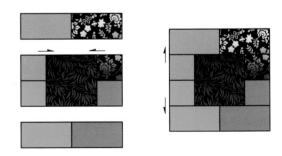

**5** Repeat steps 2–4 to make four blocks of each of the color combinations shown, for a total of 20 blocks.

Make 4 of each.

## ASSEMBLING THE QUILT TOP

**1** Using a design wall or other flat surface, arrange the completed blocks into five rows of four blocks each as shown in the quilt layout diagram.

**2** Sew the blocks into rows, pressing seam allowances in opposite directions from row to row. Sew the rows together and press.

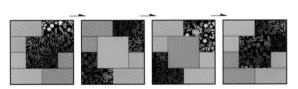

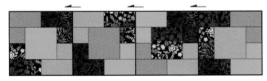

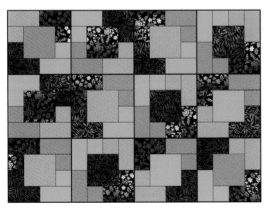

## FINISHING

**1** Refer to "Completing the Quilt" on page 76 to layer the quilt top, batting, and backing. Quilt as desired.

**2** Sew the 2½" x 15" binding strips together to form one continuous strip and bind the quilt.

# PICKS a basket of blooms

Designed by Kathy Brown; pieced by Linda Reed; quilted by Carol Hilton

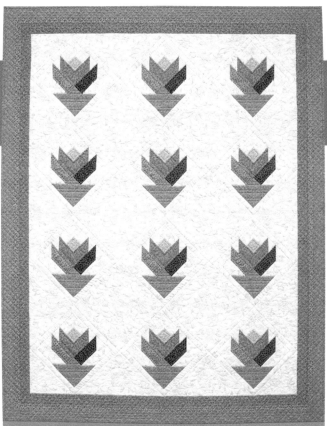

# By now it's quite

evident that I grew up as a tomboy, rarely taking a shine to girlie things. But there were exceptions every now and then. We had a small flowerbed next to the driveway of our home where my mom planted four-o'clocks. I was always fascinated by the tiny little buds that would appear each afternoon, only to blossom into full flowers as the afternoon wore on, and then fade away with the morning dew. The buds in these Basket blocks remind me of those four-o'clocks and the delight I had in watching them bloom!

## MATERIALS

*Yardage is based on 42"-wide fabric.*

½ yard of blue print for blocks

⅜ yard of dark-pink tone-on-tone fabric for blocks

¼ yard of light-green leaf print for blocks

¼ yard of dark-green leaf print for blocks

⅛ yard of light-pink tone-on-tone fabric for blocks

3½ yards of pink-and-white toile for blocks and setting triangles

⅔ yard of dark-pink print for inner border

½ yard of light-green leaf print for middle border

1½ yards of blue print for outer border and binding

5 yards of fabric for backing

69" x 86" piece of batting

## CUTTING

**From the light-pink tone-on-tone fabric, cut:**

12 squares, 2½" x 2½"

**From the dark-pink tone-on-tone fabric, cut:**

4 strips, 2½" x 42"; crosscut into:

    12 rectangles, 2½" x 6½"

    12 rectangles, 2½" x 4½"

**From the light-green leaf print for blocks, cut:**

2 strips, 2½" x 42"; crosscut into 12 rectangles, 2½" x 6½"

**From the dark-green leaf print, cut:**

2 strips, 2½" x 42"; crosscut into 12 rectangles, 2½" x 6½"

**From the blue print for blocks, cut:**

2 strips, 2½" x 42"; crosscut into 24 squares, 2½" x 2½"

2 strips, 4½" x 42"; crosscut into 12 squares, 4½" x 4½"

**From the pink-and-white toile, cut:**

6 squares, 12½" x 12½"

2 squares, 9⅜" x 9⅜"; cut each square in half diagonally to yield 4 corner setting triangles

3 squares, 18¼" x 18¼"; cut each square into quarters diagonally to yield 12 side setting triangles (2 are extra)

9 strips, 2½" x 42"; crosscut into:

    84 squares, 2½" x 2½"

    24 rectangles, 2½" x 6½"

16 strips, 1½" x 42"; crosscut into:

    24 rectangles, 1½" x 10½"

    24 rectangles, 1½" x 12½"

**From the dark-pink print for inner border, cut:**

8 strips, 2½" x 42"

**From the light-green leaf print for middle border, cut:**

8 strips, 1½" x 42"

**From the blue print for outer border and binding, cut:**

16 strips, 2½" x 42"

## CONSTRUCTING THE BLOCKS

1. Separate the fabrics, stacking all of the same-fabric rectangles and squares into groups so that you have six different groupings: light-pink tone-on-tone fabric, dark-pink tone-on-tone fabric, light-green leaf print, dark-green leaf print, blue print, and pink-and-white toile.

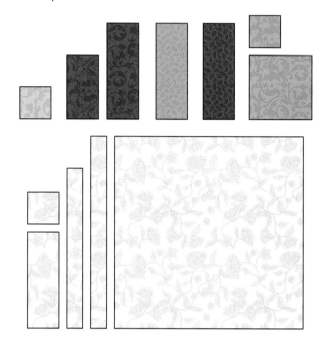

2. Draw a diagonal line from corner to corner on the wrong side of 48 of the pink-and-white toile 2½" squares.

3. Place a marked pink-and-white toile square right sides together with a dark-pink tone-on-tone 2½" x 4½" rectangle so that the diagonal line is oriented as shown. Sew on the drawn line. Trim the excess ¼" from the sewn line, and fold back the triangle. Press. Make 12 of these pieced units. Repeat to make 12 pieced units using the light-green leaf print 2½" x 6½" rectangles.

Make 12.   Make 12.

**4** Place a marked pink-and-white toile 2½" square right sides together with a dark-pink tone-on-tone 2½" x 6½" rectangle so that the diagonal line is going in the opposite direction of the units from step 3 as shown. Sew on the drawn line, trim, and press as before. Make 12 of these pieced rectangles. Repeat with the dark-green 2½" x 6½" rectangles to make 12 dark-green pieced rectangles.

Make 12.    Make 12.

**5** Draw a diagonal line from corner to corner on the wrong side of the blue-print 2½" squares and sew them to the pink-and-white toile 2½" x 6½" rectangles in the same manner to make a total of 24 pieced rectangles as shown.

Make 12.    Make 12.

**6** Arrange and sew three pink-and-white toile 2½" squares and one light-pink 2½" square together as shown.

**7** Sew a dark-pink pieced 2½" x 4½" rectangle to the left side of the unit from step 6. Sew a dark-pink pieced 2½" x 6½" rectangle to the bottom.

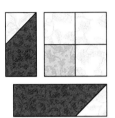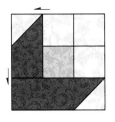

**8** Sew a light-green pieced rectangle to a pink-and-white toile pieced rectangle as shown. Sew this unit to the left side of the unit from step 7.

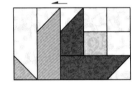

**9** Sew units from steps 4 and 5 together with a blue 4½" square as shown.

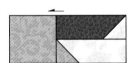

**10** Join the units from steps 8 and 9 as shown.

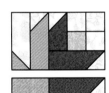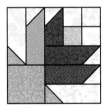

**11** Sew pink-and-white toile 1½" x 10½" rectangles to the top and bottom of the unit from step 10. Press. Sew a 1½" x 12½" rectangle to each side of the unit. Press.

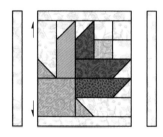 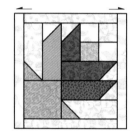

**12** Repeat steps 6–11 to make 12 blocks.

## ASSEMBLING THE QUILT TOP

**1** Using a design wall or other flat surface, arrange the completed blocks in diagonal rows with the pink-and-white toile setting squares and triangles as shown in the quilt layout diagram.

**2** Sew the blocks and side setting triangles into diagonal rows. Press the seam allowances toward the setting blocks and triangles. Sew the rows together and add the corner triangles last.

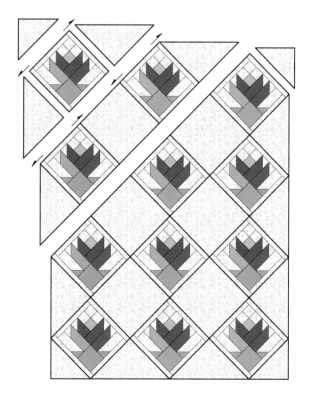

**3** Referring to "Adding Borders" on page 76, sew two dark-pink inner-border strips together to make one long strip. Repeat to make four long strips.

**4** Sew the inner borders to the quilt top. Press.

**5** Repeat steps 3 and 4 to add the middle and outer borders.

## FINISHING

**1** Refer to "Completing the Quilt" on page 76 to layer the quilt top, batting, and backing. Quilt as desired.

**2** Sew the binding strips together to form one continuous strip and bind the quilt.

# quiltmaking BASICS

Creating successful Take 5 quilts requires a few basic supplies and a familiarity with simple quilting techniques. If you're a beginner, follow the guidelines throughout this section as you construct your quilts.

## MATERIALS

If you're already a quilter, you probably have most of these tools and supplies on hand. If you're new to quilting, these basic items will be enough to get started.

- Good-quality, 100% cotton fabrics
- Thread in a neutral color
- Rotary cutter
- 24" x 36" rotary-cutting mat
- 6½" x 24½" acrylic ruler
- Self-adhesive ruler grip dots or Invisi-Grip (to keep your ruler from slipping)
- Glass-head silk pins
- Quilters' pins
- Seam ripper
- A sewing machine in good working order with a ¼" presser foot

## ROTARY CUTTING

Since rotary cutting is covered in so many quilting books, I won't go into great detail on how to use a rotary cutter. What you do need to remember as you begin each new project in this book is to start with a new rotary-cutter blade. You'll be cutting through multiple layers of fabric and will need the sharp, accurate edge that a new blade provides.

❶ Open each cut of fabric and press out the center fold. I prefer to starch the fabrics at this time so that I get a more accurate cut, but this is a personal preference.

❷ With the fabrics open, lay each one down on your cutting mat, one on top of the other. Place a selvage edge on the left and the other selvage edge on the right. Lay the 6½" x 24½" ruler over the left edge. Check to make sure that all layers of fabric are showing underneath the ruler and that you'll be trimming off all of the selvages.

❸ Using a rotary cutter, cut along the right edge of the ruler. Slide the ruler upward as you reach the end of it, keeping the edge of the ruler aligned with the cut edge of the fabric. Discard the selvages.

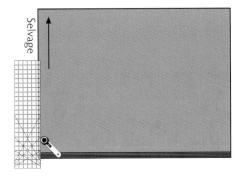

❹ Rotate the fabric or reposition your body so that the newly cut edge is closest to you. Align the short end of the ruler with the straightened edge of the fabric stack, and again check to make sure that all layers of fabric are visible before cutting. Using a rotary cutter, trim the raw edges of the fabric stack.

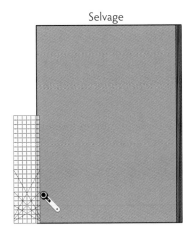

**❺** Having made these edges square, you're ready to begin cutting your fabrics. Follow the cutting guides included in each quilt project to make the individual cuts. Repeat steps 2 and 3 to restraighten the edges after you've made several cuts, or if the layers shift while cutting.

*Note:* If your fabric pieces are larger than the size of your rotary-cutting mat, you'll need to make the initial cuts that fall on top of the mat, then gently slide the remainder of the fabric stack onto the mat and continue cutting. If any of the fabric stack shifted in the move, simply re-square the left and bottom edges with your ruler and rotary cutter before resuming cutting.

## PINNING AND PRESSING

To pin or not to pin is an issue that most quilters face at some point during their quilting journey. I've found through much trial, error, and angst that it's far better to take the time to pin. Your blocks will be more likely to go together with accurate intersecting points, and you'll avoid ripping the blocks apart later when they don't fit together properly. If you choose not to pin, that's your personal choice, but don't say I didn't urge you to do so!

Accurate pressing is a must in my opinion. As with pinning, I find that my blocks fit together better and are much straighter if I press each seam after sewing it.

## ADDING BORDERS

Not all of the quilts in this book have borders, but those that do feature simple butted corners—no mitering or complex measuring is involved. Cut border strips across the width of the fabric and piece them when needed to achieve the required length.

To piece the border strips, place the ends of the strips right sides together at right angles as shown. Sew diagonally from the point where the strips meet at the top of the horizontal strip to the point where the strips meet at the bottom of the horizontal strip. Trim ¼" from the stitching line and press the seam allowances open.

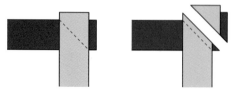

To add the borders to the quilt, mark the center points of each edge of the quilt top. Mark the center point on one long edge of each border strip. With right sides together, pin the left and right border strips to the quilt top, matching the center marks. There will be excess border fabric extending beyond the quilt top. Stitch the borders in place, and then trim the excess even with the top and bottom of the quilt top. Press the seam allowances toward the border strips. Repeat for the top and bottom borders, trimming the excess even with the sides of the quilt top.

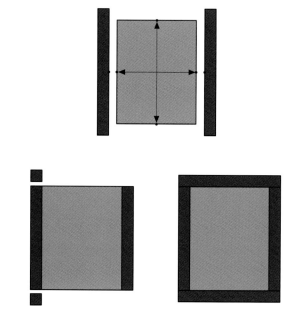

## COMPLETING THE QUILT

When the quilt top is pieced, you can move on to the final steps to finish your quilt.

### Layering and Quilting

Before the quilting begins, prepare the batting and backing so that they're at least 4" wider and longer than the quilt top. The fabric requirements in each project have allowed for this excess. Layer the batting between the backing and the quilt top, and baste the layers together with pins for machine quilting or thread for hand quilting. Quilt as desired.

All of the quilts in this book were quilted on a long-arm quilting machine, but you can certainly use any quilting method that you prefer. If someone else will be doing the quilting, be sure to check with the quilter regarding the backing size and preparation of your quilt top.

## Binding

I used traditional double-fold binding for all of the quilts in this book. I make a continuous length of binding with strips that are cut 2½" wide. All yardage amounts are based on 2½"-wide strips cut across the width of the fabric.

1 Join binding strips with a diagonal seam, in the same manner as for border strips (see page 76) to make one long strip.

2 Press the binding strip in half lengthwise with wrong sides together.

3 Leaving an 8" to 10" tail at the beginning, sew the binding to the quilt top using a ¼" seam allowance. Stop stitching ⅜" from the first corner and miter the corners as shown.

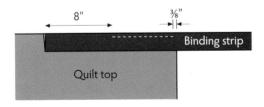

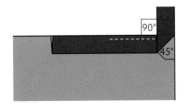

4 Stop sewing when you're about 12" from the beginning; backstitch. Overlap the end of the strip with the beginning tail. Trim the end of the binding strip so that it overlaps by 2½" (or the width that you cut your binding). Place the binding ends together at right angles and sew the ends together on the diagonal as shown. Trim, leaving a ¼" seam allowance. Press the seam allowances open. Reposition the binding on the quilt and finish sewing.

Overlapped ends

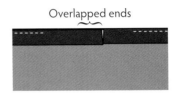

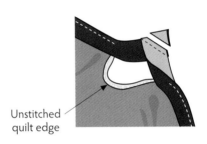

Unstitched quilt edge

5 Fold the binding to the back of the quilt and hand stitch it in place, mitering the corners. To make it easier to fold the binding over, I add spray starch to the binding and press it toward the raw edges of the quilt.

# acknowledgments

With a grateful heart, I give warm thanks to:

My husband, for everything from stuffing pattern packs to cleaning house, cooking dinner, and whatever else was needed to help me meet another deadline and never uttering one word of woe!

Linda Reed for being my right arm, my brain when it fails me, my sounding board when I need it, my "everything but the kitchen sink" kind of friend. I hope you know how much I treasure our friendship. And lest I forget—thank you for the beautiful quilts you create from my designs!

The quilters of the Southern Ladies Quilting Society who helped make the gorgeous quilts in this book: Denise Bayer, Janell Crosslin, Wanda Hoffman, Andrea Keith, Yvonne Smode, and Cheryl Wilks. I'm constantly amazed at your talents and energies!

Pam Vieira-McGinnis for once again being the super woman she is and getting a quilt made in record time! I'm honored to call you my friend.

Carol Hilton for her vision in long-arm quilting. My quilts are transformed into works of art under your hands.

Debbie Bamber for hours upon hours of hand stitching the bindings on the quilts. Thank you just doesn't seem enough!

Tara Darr and Debbie Field for your gift of friendship through all these years. You both mean the world to me!

The wonderful, generous folks who supply the fabrics used in the making of these quilts: Hoffman, Moda, and Red Rooster Fabrics.

The quilters who buy my patterns, books, and fabrics: by supporting my efforts, you continue to let me live my dream of loving my work.

The quilt shops that buy my patterns, books, and fabrics: for supporting me, teaching classes from my designs, and making quilts with my fabrics. I'm honored that you consider my efforts worthy of your time and patronage.

Nancy Weber, Checker Distributors, for being such a wonderful friend as well as business associate. If it weren't for your encouragement, Take 5 would never have taken flight!

And last but not least, Karen Soltys, Cathy Reitan, Mary Burns, Karen Burns, Mary Beth Hughes, and the rest of the fabulous staff at Martingale for their help in pulling this book together. Once again, I have been privileged to have the opportunity to work with you! You girls rock!

# about the AUTHOR

It's often said that all good things come to those who wait. Well, I've never been a patient person, so this age-old adage could never have been meant for me! Yet here I sit, blessed with all the good things I could only have dreamed of: a wonderful husband whom I'm proud to call my best friend, a most extraordinary daughter and friend who graces my life each and every day, a warm and loving home filled with seven furry felines and four precious pups, and a treasure trove of amazing and caring friends who honor me with their friendship. In addition to all that, I am fortunate to have work that brings me joy and creative fulfillment on a daily basis. My jobs include:

**Author.** I certainly didn't write that into my life plan years ago, yet the kind and generous folks at Martingale saw something in me that I didn't see in myself. For that, I am ever so grateful—three times over!

**Fabric Designer.** Having always loved to create with color, I have been allowed to express that creativity through fabric design for the amazing individuals at Red Rooster Fabrics, and they have taught me so much along the way. I am honored that they have entrusted me with this gift.

**Quilter.** Of all three, this one amazes me the most. The detested sewing machine of my youth magically transformed itself into the wondrous vehicle for my creative endeavors. Go figure!

So, yes, it's often said that all good things come to those who wait. But in this fortunate girl's life, they also came because she knew how to dream—and didn't have the patience to wait! See an array of my patterns, read my blog, and learn about my workshops and lectures at www.the-teachers-pet.com.